Mystery Valley

Written by John Parsons
Illustrated by Fifi Colston

Rigby

Mystery Valley

With these characters ...

Volga

Mahar

Torda

Eru

"It was going

Setting the scene ...

In some faraway place, in some faraway time, three tired travelers stop to rest near a mysterious valley. At the end of a long day's journey, they try to settle down to sleep on the cold, hard ground. But in the valley below, mysterious events are happening. Upon investigation, the travelers meet some strange creatures and hear even stranger stories. In the morning, the travelers awake to discover that things are not as they seem . . . or are they?

o be a long, cold night."

Chapter 1

High up in the sky, a full moon shone down on the valley. It was a bitterly cold winter's night, and three tired travelers rested at the top of a hill. All around, the trees were bare. The wind blew leaves along the ground and around the travelers' feet.

The three travelers shivered. They had nowhere to stay and they felt hungry. It was going to be a long, cold night.

One of the travelers was named Mahar. He peered across the valley, looking for a light or a fire. He saw nothing, except for a long, gray river winding across the valley floor. Behind the hills, on the other side of the valley, were tall, snow-covered mountains.

"Torda! Eru!" called Mahar to the other two travelers. "How much food do we have?" Torda and Eru shook their heads. They had all been traveling for many days and there was no food left.

"We had better settle down here for the night," sighed Mahar. "Let's try and keep warm. We will get some water from the river in the morning."

The three men gathered some leaves and put them in piles. They lay down on the leaves and tried to sleep. The ground was still hard, and the wind was cold. They were hungry and tired.

After what seemed like hours of trying to fall asleep, Mahar sat up. He rubbed his eyes. He could not sleep. He sat with his chin on his knees, looking out at the moonlit valley below. Then he saw it!

Why hadn't he seen it before? How could he have missed it? Down on the valley floor, bathed in moonlight, was a huge, shining castle.

Chapter 2

From the castle walls, tiny slits of light shone out onto the valley floor. A deep red glow shone from the middle of the castle. As Mahar stood up, trying to see more of the castle, he thought he could hear music.

"Torda! Eru!" he said, nudging his sleeping friends. "Wake up!"

Torda and Eru groaned and rolled over sleepily.

"What is it?" asked Eru.

"Why did you wake us?" asked Torda.

"Look!" exclaimed Mahar. He pointed at the castle. Torda and Eru stood up quickly.

"Why didn't we see it before?" they gasped.

The three travelers grabbed their bags and hurried down the hillside. As they moved closer to the castle, they could hear music and laughter. Finally, they reached the castle gate.

Mahar banged on the gate.

"We are three cold and hungry travelers," he called out. "Please let us in."

The huge castle gate creaked and groaned and slowly swung open. Mahar, Torda, and Eru slowly and hesitantly walked inside.

Chapter 3

A strange-looking creature stood in front of the three travelers. He had a small body and a huge head with long pointy ears. He looked at the three travelers and smiled.

"Welcome!" he said. "Come and join us."

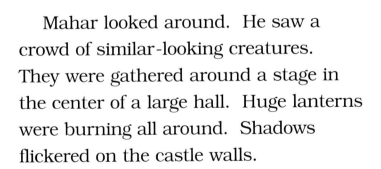

Mahar looked around. He saw a crowd of similar-looking creatures. They were gathered around a stage in the center of a large hall. Huge lanterns were burning all around. Shadows flickered on the castle walls.

"Come and join us," repeated the creature. "The dance is about to begin."

Mahar, Torda, and Eru followed the creature.

"What is your name?" asked Torda.

"My name is Volga," said the creature. "Sit here." He pointed to some soft cushions on the ground. The three travelers rested their weary bodies on the cushions. They were comfortable and warm.

"Who are . . . ," began Eru.

"Shhh!" whispered Volga. "I will tell you all about the dance as it happens."

Three creatures dressed in magnificent costumes appeared on stage. They had golden ribbons in their hair and wore brightly colored gowns. The crowd fell silent. Music sounded from behind the stage and the mysterious dance began.

"This is the story of how we came to live here," explained Volga. The three dancers moved slowly, as if they were tired.

"Many, many winters ago, our ancestors arrived at this valley. Like you, they were tired and hungry after their journey." Volga waved at someone in the crowd and another creature brought over a basket filled with freshly baked bread. "Eat," he said to Mahar, Torda, and Eru.

The dancers fell to the floor of the stage and curled up as though sleeping.

"Our ancestors could go no farther," said Volga, watching the dance. "They decided to sleep. Then, in the morning, they explored our valley. They thought it would be a good place to live. They decided to stay."

The dancers moved around the edge of the stage, looking out toward the crowd and pointing at the hills surrounding the castle. Mahar, Torda, and Eru ate the bread hungrily.

"First, our ancestors built simple houses of mud and earth, right here on the valley floor. It took them many days and nights. They dug the mud from the river bank and shaped it into bricks. They filled the gaps with earth. They covered their houses with branches that had washed up onto the edge of the river. They placed grass on the roof of each house."

The dancers moved gracefully and busily, pretending to build mud houses. When they had finished, they sat down in a circle and looked pleased with themselves.

Then they leaped to their feet and started to run wildly around the stage, shaking their heads. They looked up at the sky and danced even faster.

"What's happening?" whispered Mahar.

"One terrible night, when everyone was asleep, a fierce storm came over the valley. It rained and rained. The water poured down the hillsides and into the river. The river rose until water was spilling over the banks. It continued to rain and the river swirled around the mud houses. The rain started to soak through the grass roofs. Eventually, the houses began to crumble. By the morning, they had all washed away."

The dancers stopped suddenly and dropped to the ground. The music stopped and strange wailing sounds came from the crowd.

Chapter 4

Mahar, Torda, and Eru sat staring at the stage. Slowly, the dancers started to move again. They picked themselves up slowly and moved as if they were tired and hungry again. They leaned forward, as though they were climbing a hill.

"Our ancestors moved up to the hills surrounding the valley floor," said Volga. "They had learned that houses made of mud and earth would not last next to a river. They decided to gather twigs, sticks, and branches. Then, they started to build houses using better materials in a safer place."

The dancers on stage pretended to build again. Mahar, Torda, and Eru imagined stronger, bigger houses made of wood being built on the hillside. The rhythm of the music became stronger and faster, and the dancers started to smile again. One of the creatures from the crowd carried a big plate of tasty cheeses over to Volga, and he offered it to his new friends.

"Please, help yourselves. We have plenty."

"The wooden houses were warmer," Volga went on. "The hillside was a pleasant place to live and our ancestors were happy. They planted crops in the springtime and waited for summer to arrive."

The dancers crouched down and slowly began to rise up again, their arms spread out wide. They were pretending to be the seedlings of the crops, rising up in the sunlight, growing tall and strong. The crowd cheered and the music was joyful. Then, suddenly, someone banged on a huge drum. A loud boom echoed around the castle walls. The crowd fell silent. Mahar, Torda, and Eru stopped eating.

"Just as the crops were ready for harvest, an awful thunderstorm struck."

"Huge bolts of lightning came down from the sky. The lightning struck the trees on the hillside. Blazing branches fell to the ground, starting a terrible fire on the hillside."

Once more, the dancers ran around the stage wildly, shaking their heads and flapping their arms.

They circled closer and closer to the middle of the stage, until they all huddled together and fell to the floor.

"The forest fire was very fierce. The fire swept through our ancestors' village, burning all the houses."

"The crops were ruined and all that remained were ashes. It was a disaster." Volga looked very sad.

The crowd started to wail again, as the music got louder and louder. Then everyone was suddenly quiet when they heard a louder beat of the drum. Mahar, Torda, and Eru could not take their eyes off the stage.

Chapter 5

Volga looked at Mahar, Torda, and Eru.

"Our ancestors did not give up.
They saved what they could from the
ashes and headed for the mountains.
Up there, high above the valley, surely
they would be safe. There were no
rivers to wash away their houses and
no forest fires to burn their houses."

Mahar, Torda, and Eru watched
as the dancers moved their hands
through the imaginary ashes. Then,
once more, they slowly picked
themselves up from the floor, leaned
forward, and slowly, wearily danced on.

"It was colder in the mountains," said Volga. "Even at the end of summer, there was still snow, high up where our ancestors stopped. They could see that, even in the sunshine, the mountains were so high that the snow did not melt. They decided that they would build their houses from ice and snow. After the last disaster, they wanted to be sure that nothing would burn. Would you like some fruit?"

The three travelers nodded, their eyes still fixed on the stage.

The dancers blew on their hands and rubbed them together to keep warm. They moved across the stage as they pretended to move huge blocks of ice.

Mahar, Torda, and Eru imagined beautiful igloos being built high up on the mountainside. They knew that, even though they were made of frozen ice and snow, igloos were warm inside. They trapped all the heat and protected the people inside from the freezing winds.

"Eventually, the ice town was completed. It was brilliant in the sunshine, sparkling blue, white, and green. In the evenings, the sunsets would glow orange and red through the ice. Our ancestors were happy here."

Volga smiled and bit into a huge, red apple. The dancers sat resting in a circle, gazing at the sky. They smiled and were contented again. The crowd clapped and the music played cheerfully. Then another instrument began to play, so quietly that the three travelers could hardly hear it at first. It was a tiny pair of cymbals.

"The summer turned to fall, and the fall turned to winter," said Volga, as he finished eating his apple.

"The weather became colder and soon it began to snow on the mountain-side. The ancestors were happy in their ice town, and the snow did not bother them. It snowed and snowed and snowed. Before long, all the houses had three feet of snow on top of them. They looked like upside-down snow-covered ice cream cones."

A bigger pair of cymbals took over from the tiny cymbals, hissing and crashing, louder and louder.  Volga's eyes widened and looked sad.

"What our ancestors did not know was that on the very top of the mountain, the snow was getting too heavy."

"After many days of snow, a huge weight had collected on the mountain-top. Then, without warning, one night it started to move. An avalanche had begun!"

The cymbals were bashing and crashing so loud that everyone in the crowd had their hands over their long, pointy ears. They started to wail again and the dancers fell to the floor of the stage. They were rolling around and around, faster and faster.

"The avalanche hurtled down the mountainside and the snow swept away the igloos and everything in them. It was another disaster. There was only one thing that our ancestors could do."

"Build this castle?" asked Eru.

"Yes," replied Volga. "But they had to build a castle that would never be washed away. They had to build a castle that would never catch fire. They had to build a castle that would never be swept down a mountainside. They had to design a castle that would be able to stand up to *any* disaster. They had to build a castle that would last forever!"

Mahar nodded and looked at the stage. He was surprised to see that it was empty. The lanterns had gone out and the crowd had disappeared. They were alone with Volga, in the middle of the dark, deserted castle.

Chapter 6

"Where is everyone?" asked Mahar. Volga smiled and yawned.

"We are all tired," he said. "A lot of work goes into this one night of the year when we perform the story of our ancestors. It is time to sleep."

Torda was about to ask what Volga meant about the "one night", but he suddenly felt tired too. Mahar and Eru were yawning. Volga brought out soft feather mattresses and the three travelers lay down to sleep. He smiled when Mahar, Torda, and Eru thanked him for the food and the shelter.

"I have a feeling we will see you next year," smiled Volga. He turned and disappeared into the darkness.

The three travelers fell asleep quickly, feeling warm, comfortable, and well fed.

Mahar woke when the morning sun started to shine on his face. He stretched and remembered the dancing from the night before. He rolled over, wanting to snuggle into his soft, warm mattress for another few minutes' sleep. But the mattress felt hard and cold.

He opened his eyes. He was back on the hillside with the bare trees. He was covered in damp leaves. He sat up and blinked. He stared out over the valley. There was nothing there—only a cold, gray river winding across the valley floor. There was no castle.

Mahar stood up and shook the leaves off his clothes. At first he was sad. But then he laughed.

"A dream," he said. "It was all just a dream." He nudged Torda and Eru. "Wake up, you two. We need to continue our journey."

Torda and Eru groaned. Eru rolled over and Torda rubbed his eyes.

"I wonder what Volga will bring us for breakfast?" Torda asked, yawning.

"I don't want any breakfast," groaned Eru. "I want another one of these soft feather mattresses."

Mahar stared at his two friends.

"You dreamed it as well?" he gasped. "You dreamed about the castle?"

"What dream?" asked Torda. He opened his eyes and blinked.

He looked surprised by what he saw.
Eru opened his eyes and looked in
dismay at the leaves surrounding him.

"What happened to the castle? The
dancers? My mattress?" he exclaimed.

Mahar, Torda, and Eru all stood up
and looked at each other.

"Did we all dream the same dream?"
they asked.

Mahar nodded.

"It must have been the cold conditions and our tiredness," he said. "And although the dream was nice, we are still here. And we still have no food and a long way to travel."

Torda and Eru looked very unhappy. They sighed and started to gather their things. The cold wind blew across the hill. Clouds gathered along the edge of the mountains.

Just as they were about to leave, Mahar spotted something under a pile of leaves. He called out to Torda and Eru.

"It doesn't belong to us," they said. "We have everything."

Mahar moved forward to take a closer look. His eyes grew wide as he uncovered a small basket.

He held his breath. The other two crouched down beside him, looking amazed. Mahar carefully lifted the lid of the basket. All three gasped when they saw what was inside. A loaf of freshly baked bread, some cheese, and some apples. And hidden among the food was a tiny piece of paper, with a message written in strange letters:

"I WISH YOU ALL A SAFE JOURNEY. HAVE YOU GUESSED THAT ONLY A CASTLE BUILT OF DREAMS CAN STAND UP TO ANY DISASTER? I HAVE A FEELING WE WILL SEE YOU NEXT YEAR! V."

"A castle of dreams."

To travel is to
Reach out to
Another place
Visit us here
Enter our world
Leave us with dreams to tell.